Published By Robert Corbin

SOUTH BEACH DIET

The Updated, Easy And Delicious Faster Weight Loss Plan

For Healthy And Improved Health

Published By Robert Corbin

@ Dan Clark

South Beach Diet: The Updated, Easy And Delicious Faster Weight Loss Plan For Healthy And Improved Health

All Right RESERVED

ISBN 978-87-94477-99-4

TABLE OF CONTENTS

Chockfull Of Veggie Chili 1

Spinach & Artichoke Stuffed Chicken Breast 4

Mexican Omelet 7

Scrambled Mozzarella Eggs 9

Cannellini Bean Salad 11

Blueberry Muffin Cake 13

Pecan Cookie 15

Asparagus Cauliflower Hash 17

Taco Style Lettuce Wraps 19

Awesome Chicken Stew 21

Greek Salad... 23

Turkey Avocado Sandwich.. 25

Blt Lettuce Wraps 26

Weight-Loss Cabbage Soup 27

Tomato-&-Avocado Cheese Sandwich 29

Spanish Chicken And Beans.. 31

Grilled Lemon Garlic Chicken With Roasted Vegetables 34

Baked Salmon With Asparagus And Quinoa 36

Grilled Chicken Breast With Roasted Vegetables........... 38

Baked Salmon With Lemon And Dill................................ 40

Lemon Garlic Grilled Shrimp.. 42

Bacon, Avocado And Jack Cheese Omelet With Salsa.... 44

Scrambled Eggs... 47

Beef Huevos Rancheros.. 49

2-Step Chia Yogurt.. 52

Spanish Braised Chicken In Creamy Almond Sauce........ 54

H Omemade Calzone With Cauliflower Crust 57

Chocolate Peanut Butter Mug Muffins 60

Southern Stuffed Eggs 62

Trattoria Frittata.. 64

Lentil Soup.. 65

Rare Roast Beef Salad With Mustard Mayonnaise From Amy Kanarios.. 69

Broccoli, Bacon, And Cheese Quiche............................... 72

Granola 74

Cauliflower Mac And Cheese 76

Breakfast Mix 77

Sausage Breakfast Sandwich 78

Strawberry Yogurt 79

Delicious Baked Garlic Salmon Filets 81

Egg Muffins 83

Grilled Chicken Caesar Salad Wrap 85

Veggie Hummus Wrap 86

Homemade Protein Bars 87

Roasted Red Pepper Dip 89

Chicken With Mushroom And Leeks 91

Lime And Potato Coconut Curry With Fish 94

Baked Chicken With Sweet Potato 97

Mediterranean Chickpea Salad: 98

Spinach And Mozzarella Frittata 101

Peanut Butter And Jelly Cookies 103

Vegetable And Chickpea Curry 106

Cauliflower And Broccoli Soup 108

Turkey And Vegetable Skewers 110

- Fried Eggs And Vegetables 112
- Cheesy Tuna Casserole 114
- Baby Spinach Omelet 116
- 1-Minute Chocolate Ricotta Mousse 118
- No-Bake Strawberry Cheesecake Bliss Balls 119
- Instant Pot Keto Tuscan Soup 121
- Lobster Salad In Endive Guacamole Dip Or Salad Dressing 124
- Lentil Soup 126
- Rare Roast Beef Salad With Mustard Mayonnaise From Amy Kanarios 129
- Caribbean Chicken Salad 132
- Balsamic And Bacon Vegetable Medley 135
- Garden Vegetable Soup 137
- French Onion Soup 138
- Raspberry Crumble 140

Chockfull Of Veggie Chili

Ingredients:s:

- ½ cup bell peppers, diced
- 1 Tbsp. minced garlic
- 1 tsp. paprika
- ½ tsp. chili powder
- ½ cup diced tomatoes
- ½ cup chicken broth
- ¼ cup canned kidney beans, rinsed and drained ¼ cup shelled edamame
- ¾ cup veggie crumbles (finished soy protein) 2 Tbsp. scallions, chopped
- 2 Tbsp. olive oil
- ¼ cup onion, diced

- ¼ cup carrots, diced
- ¼ cup celery, diced
- ½ cup zucchini, diced
- Salt and pepper, to taste

Directions:s:

1. Heat olive oil in a large saucepan over medium heat.
2. Add the onions, carrots, celery and salt and pepper to taste. Cook for 3-4 minutes, until the onions are translucent.
3. Add the zucchini and bell peppers . Cook for 2-3 minutes.
4. Add the garlic, paprika and chili powder. Cook for 1 moment, until fragrant. Add the diced tomatoes and stock to the pot and stir to consolidate.
5. Add the kidney beans, edamame and veggie crumbles .

6. Bring the mixture to a boil and then reduce the hotness to low. Stew for 8-10 minutes, until somewhat thickened.
7. Divide chili evenly between 2 bowls and garnish with chopped scallions before serving.

Spinach & Artichoke Stuffed Chicken Breast

Ingredients:s:

- 1/4" thickness 2 Tbsp. extra virgin olive oil

- 2cloves garlic, sliced

- 1 cup chicken broth

- 2 Tbsp. lemon juice

- 1 tsp. sea salt

- 1 tsp. ground black pepper

- 1 Tbsp. chopped basil

- ½ cup frozen spinach, thawed and hacked

- 1 cup mozzarella cheese, shredded

- ½ cup marinated artichoke hearts, chopped

- ½ cup marinated artichoke hearts, chopped

- 3 oz. boneless, skinless chicken breasts, beat to

Directions:s:

1. Preheat the stove to 350°F.
2. In a bowl, consolidate spinach, artichoke hearts and cheese to make the filling.
3. Top half of each entire bosom equally with spinach mixture. Crease half of the chicken over the filling and fasten the edges with wooden picks.
4. Heat the oil in a large skillet over medium - high heat. Add the garlic and cook for 3 minutes.
5. Add the chicken bosoms to the skillet and cook for 7 minutes per side, or until all around cooked on both sides.
6. Remove the chicken breasts and place them in an oven -proof dish.

7. Bake for 30 minutes, or until a thermometer inserted in the thickest portion registers 170°F and the juices run clear.
8. While the chicken is baking, add the broth, lemon juice, salt and pepper the large skillet.
9. Heat to boiling. Reduce the hotness to low, cover and stew for 20 minutes.
10. To serve, remove and discard the wooden picks. Arrange the chicken on a warm serving platter and spoon the sauce over the chicken.

Mexican Omelet

Ingredients:s:

- 3/4 C. chopped avocado
- 1/3 C. sour cream
- 2 T. chopped green chile
- 1 T. chopped scallion
- 1 tsp. lemon juice
- 1/4 tsp. salt
- Dash of Tabasco sauce
- 2 T. butter or margarine
- 6 beaten eggs
- 1 C. shredded Monterey Jack cheese

Directions:s:

1. In a small bowl, combine the first 7 ingredients. In a 10?inch ovenproof skillet, melt the butter over medium heat pour eggs into the skillet and cook 3 to 5 minutes, lifting eggs to allow the uncooked portion to flow underneath.
2. Remove from heat; sprinkle egg evenly with cheese and place skillet in a 325ºF oven for 3 to 4 minutes or until the cheese melts.
3. Spread avocado mixture on top 1/2 omelet and return it to the oven for 5 to 7 minutes. Fold the omelet in half to serve.

Scrambled Mozzarella Eggs

Ingredients:s:

- 6 extra large eggs

- 1/4 tsp. salt

- 1/8 tsp. pepper

- 1/4 lb low fat mozzarella cheese, coarsely shredded

Directions:s:

1. Preheat oven to 350ºF. Put butter in a 9?inch round metal cake pan in the oven just long enough to melt but not brown; remove and swirl butter to coat bottom and sides of pan.
2. Beat eggs, milk, salt and pepper to blend. Pour into prepared pan and place in oven.
3. When mixture begins to set, in about 5 minutes, draw a large spoon or spatula

around sides and bottom of the pan to form large curds.
4. Repeat process at 1 minute intervals for 2 or 3 times, depending on how set you want eggs.
5. Remove from pan with sweeping motions of the spoon or spatula, and fold in mozzarella. Serve at once!

Cannellini Bean Salad

Ingredients:s:

Dressing:

- Pinch of oregano
- 1 clove garlic, slightly broken
- 1 cup olive oil
- 2 1/3 cup red wine vinegar
- Salt & pepper to taste

Salad:

- 2 cans cannellini beans
- 2 red onions, chopped
- 1 bell pepper
- Minced parsley

Directions:s:

1. Dressing: Mix all ingredients together and let set at room temperature toblend flavors.
2. Salad: Drain 2 cans of cannellini beans and rinse under cold water. Place in bowl and add 2 red onion chopped, 1 bell pepper cut in small pieces and some minced parsley.
3. Add the dressing and adjust the salt and pepper. Add a little more oregano, if desired.

Blueberry Muffin Cake

Ingredients:

- 1½ teaspoons baking powder

- 1 teaspoon vanilla extract

- ½ teaspoon baking soda

- ¼ teaspoon salt

- 3 cups almond flour

- ½ cup 2% fat plain Greek yogurt

- ¼ cup powdered erythritol sweetener of your choice

- 3 large eggs

- 2 to 3 teaspoons grated lemon zest

- 1 cup fresh or frozen blueberries

Directions:

1. Coat a slow cooker generously with cooking spray.
2. In a large bowl, mix together the almond flour, yogurt, erythritol, eggs, lemon zest, baking powder, vanilla, baking soda, and salt until well blended.
3. Carefully fold in the blueberries.
4. Pour the batter into the slow cooker.
5. Place a paper towel between the slow cooker and the lid to cut down on any condensation that develops.
6. Cook on low for 4 to 6 hours or on high for 2 to 3 hours, or until a toothpick inserted in the center comes out clean.

Pecan Cookie

Ingredients:

- 1 large egg
- 5 tablespoons unsalted butter, at room temperature
- 1 tablespoon coconut flour
- 1 teaspoon baking powder
- 1¼ cup almond flour
- ⅔ cup powdered erythritol sweetener of your choice
- ⅓ cup chopped pecans
- ½ teaspoon vanilla extract

Directions:

1. Coat a slow cooker generously with cooking spray.

2. In a large bowl, mix together the almond flour, erythritol, pecans, egg, butter, coconut flour, baking powder, and vanilla until well blended. Pour the batter into the slow cooker.
3. Place a paper towel between the slow cooker and the lid to cut down on any condensation that develops.
4. Cook on low for 4 to 6 hours or on high for 2 to 3 hours, or until a toothpick inserted in the center comes out clean.

Asparagus Cauliflower Hash

Ingredients:

- 1 teaspoon salt
- ¼ teaspoon freshly ground black pepper
- 1 medium head cauliflower, shredded or riced
- 12 large eggs
- ½ cup low-fat 1% milk
- 2 cups shredded part-skim mozzarella cheese
- 1 pound asparagus, chopped

Directions:
1. Coat a slow cooker generously with cooking spray.
2. In a large bowl, whisk together the eggs, milk, cheese, salt, and pepper.

3. Add half the cauliflower to the bottom of the slow cooker. Top with half the asparagus. Repeat with the remaining cauliflower and asparagus.
4. Pour the eggs into the slow cooker.
5. Cook on low for 6 to 8 hours or on high for 3 to 4 hours, or until eggs are set.

Taco Style Lettuce Wraps

Ingredients:

- 1 medium diced fresh tomato
- ½ cup low fat cottage cheese
- 1 Tbsp. olive oil
- 4 large lettuce leaves (romaine lettuce or other of your choice)
- 1-pound lean turkey meat
- ¼ diced red onion
- Fresh minced cilantro

Directions:
1. In a large skillet, heat the oil and sautéed the red onion for a few minutes before adding the ground meat.

2. Cook the meat for about 20 minutes, kept stirring to make sure it stays rumbly.
3. Meanwhile, prepare the lettuce, plate and add a full tablespoon of cottage cheese in each.
4. When the meat is fully cooked, add some in each leaf-wrap and sprinkle some fresh tomatoes and fresh chopped cilantro on it.

Awesome Chicken Stew

Ingredients:

- 1 cup low fat vegetables broth
- 1 tbsp. white balsamic vinegar
- 2 tbsp. agave syrup
- 1 tsp. chili powder
- 1 tsp. red pepper flakes
- 1 Tbsp. lemon juice
- ½ tsp. cumin
- 1 tbsp. olive oil
- 3 large cooked and shredded chicken breasts
- 1 small chopped yellow onion
- 2 minced garlic cloves

- 1 large can dice tomatoes with chilies
- Salt, black pepper

Directions:
1. I always opt to use the crockpot for this recipe, I think it's just easier.
2. Use chicken you cooked previously and shred it.
3. In a skillet, heat the oil and cook the garlic and onions for about 5 minutes.
4. Then in the crockpot, add all the veggies, including the tomatoes, the broth, the cooked chicken, vinegar and all spices.
5. Stir and set om low temperature for 4 hours.
6. When you are ready to serve, add some of your favorite toppings as suggested above.

Greek Salad

Ingredients:

- 1/2 cup cherry tomatoes, halved
- 1/4 cup Kalamata olives, pitted
- 1/4 cup feta cheese, crumbled
- 2 tbsp olive oil
- 2 tbsp red wine vinegar
- 2 cups mixed greens
- 1/2 cucumber, sliced
- 1/2 red onion, sliced
- Salt and pepper to taste

Directions:

1. Place mixed greens in a large bowl.

2. Add cucumber, red onion, cherry tomatoes, Kalamata olives, and feta cheese.
3. Drizzle with olive oil and red wine vinegar.
4. Season with salt and pepper to taste.

Turkey Avocado Sandwich

Ingredients:

- 1/4 cup mixed greens
- 1 tbsp Dijon mustard
- 2 slices whole wheat bread
- 4 oz sliced turkey breast
- 1/4 avocado, sliced
- Salt and pepper to taste

Directions:
1. Toast bread slices.
2. Spread Dijon mustard on one slice of bread.
3. Layer turkey breast, avocado, and mixed greens on top of the Dijon mustard.
4. Season with salt and pepper to taste.
5. Top with the other slice of bread.

Blt Lettuce Wraps

Ingredients:

- 1/2 cup cherry tomatoes, halved
- 1/4 cup mayonnaise
- 1 tbsp lemon juice
- 4-6 large lettuce leaves
- 4-6 slices bacon, cooked and crumbled
- Salt and pepper to taste

Directions:

1. Wash and dry lettuce leaves.
2. In a medium bowl, mix together bacon, cherry tomatoes, mayonnaise, and lemon juice.
3. Season with salt and pepper to taste.
4. Spoon the bacon mixture onto lettuce leaves.
5. Roll up the lettuce leaves and serve.

Weight-Loss Cabbage Soup

Ingredients:

- 2 cloves garlic, minced
- 1½ teaspoons Italian seasoning
- ½ teaspoon ground pepper
- ¼ teaspoon salt
- 8 cups low-sodium vegetable broth
- 1 medium head green cabbage, halved and sliced
- 1 large tomato, chopped
- 2 tablespoons extra-virgin olive oil
- 1 medium onion, chopped
- 2 medium carrots, chopped
- 2 stalks celery, chopped

- 1 medium red bell pepper, chopped

- 2 teaspoons white-wine vinegar

Directions:
1. Heat oil in a large pot over medium heat.
2. Add onion, carrots and celery.
3. Cook, stirring, until the vegetables begin to soften, 6 to 8 minutes.
4. Add bell pepper, garlic, Italian seasoning, pepper and salt and cook, stirring, for 2 minutes.
5. Add broth, cabbage and tomato; increase heat to medium-high and bring to a boil.
6. Reduce heat to maintain a simmer, partially cover and cook until all the vegetables are tender, 15 to 20 minutes more.
7. Remove from heat and stir in vinegar.
8. Feast!

Tomato-&-Avocado Cheese Sandwich

Ingredients:

- 3 slices tomato
- ¼ cup grated Parmesan cheese
- 1 cup mixed salad greens or baby spinach
- 2 teaspoons balsamic vinegar
- 2 slices whole-wheat bread
- ¼ avocado, mashed
- 1 medium ripe pear

Directions:
1. Lay bread on work surface. Spread avocado on one slice. Top with tomatoes and sprinkle with cheese.
2. Toast both pieces of bread in a toaster oven until the plain piece is toasted and the cheese

is starting to melt on the topped piece, 4 to 6 minutes.
3. Remove the toast from the toaster oven with a spatula, and mound greens (or spinach) on top of the cheese side.
4. Drizzle with vinegar and top with the remaining toast. Cut in half if desired and serve with pear.

Spanish Chicken And Beans

Ingredients:

- 125g green beans, chopped

- 400g can no-added-salt cannellini beans, rinsed, drained

- 1 small zucchini, sliced

- 50g (¼ cup) pitted Sicilian green olives, halved

- 400g can cherry tomatoes

- 1 tsp extra virgin olive oil

- 1 tsp smoked paprika

- 1 tsp harissa paste

- 2 garlic cloves, thinly sliced

- 1 tbsp fresh lemon juice

- 4 (about 250g) Lilydale Free Range Chicken Tenderloins

- Fresh parsley sprigs, to serve

Directions:
1. Combine paprika, harissa, garlic and lemon juice in a large sealable glass or plastic container.
2. Add chicken and turn to coat.
3. Place the green beans, cannellini beans, zucchini, olive and tomatoes in another large sealable glass or plastic container.
4. Freeze the containers for up to 3 months or until the night before cooking.
5. Defrost overnight in the fridge.
6. Heat oil in a large frying pan. Add contents of chicken container.
7. Cook for 2 minutes each side or until browned.

8. Add contents of veg container. Simmer for 10 minutes or until veg is just tender.
9. Divide chicken and veg mixture among serving plates. Top with parsley.

Grilled Lemon Garlic Chicken With Roasted Vegetables

Ingredients:

- 1 lemon, both juiced and zested
- 2 minced cloves of garlic
- 1 teaspoon of dried oregano
- 2 boneless, skinless chicken breasts
- 2 tablespoons of olive oil
- Salt and pepper to your taste
- A variety of vegetables (such as bell peppers, zucchini, and broccoli)
- Cooking spray

Directions:

1. In a mixing bowl, combine the olive oil, lemon juice, lemon zest, minced garlic,

dried oregano, and season with salt and pepper to create a marinade.
2. Place the chicken breasts into a sealable bag and pour the marinade over them. Refrigerate for at least 30 minutes.
3. Preheat your grill to medium-high heat and lightly coat the vegetables with cooking spray.
4. Grill the chicken for approximately 6-8 minutes per side until fully cooked, and grill the vegetables until they are tender and develop a slight char.
5. Serve the chicken alongside the roasted vegetables for a delicious and low-carb meal.

Baked Salmon With Asparagus And Quinoa

Ingredients:

- 2 cups of water or chicken broth
- 2 tablespoons of olive oil
- Slices of lemon
- 2 salmon filets
- 1 bunch of asparagus
- 1 cup of quinoa
- Salt and pepper to your liking

Directions:
1. Preheat your oven to 375°F (190°C).
2. Season the salmon filets with salt, pepper, and a drizzle of olive oil. Place slices of lemon on top.

3. Trim the tough ends of the asparagus and arrange them on a baking sheet. Drizzle with olive oil and season with salt and pepper.
4. Put the salmon and asparagus in the oven and bake for approximately 15-20 minutes or until the salmon easily flakes with a fork.
5. While they're baking, rinse the quinoa under cold water and combine it with water or broth in a saucepan. Bring it to a boil, then reduce the heat, cover, and simmer for around 15 minutes or until the liquid is fully absorbed.
6. Serve the oven-baked salmon and asparagus on a bed of cooked quinoa for a well-rounded and satisfying meal.

Grilled Chicken Breast With Roasted Vegetables

Ingredients:

- 1 zucchini, sliced
- 1 red onion, chopped
- 2 cloves of garlic, minced
- 2 tablespoons olive oil
- Salt and pepper to taste
- 2 boneless, skinless chicken breasts
- 1 red bell pepper, sliced
- 1 yellow bell pepper, sliced
- Fresh rosemary for garnish

Directions:

1. Preheat your grill to medium-high heat.

2. Season the chicken breasts with salt, pepper, and a drizzle of olive oil.
3. Grill the chicken for about 6-7 minutes per side, or until it reaches an internal temperature of 165°F (74°C). Remove from the grill and let it rest for a few minutes before slicing.
4. While the chicken is resting, preheat your oven to 425°F (220°C).
5. In a large bowl, toss the sliced bell peppers, zucchini, red onion, and minced garlic with olive oil, salt, and pepper.
6. Spread the seasoned vegetables on a baking sheet and roast in the preheated oven for 20-25 minutes, or until they are tender and slightly caramelized.
7. Serve the grilled chicken breast slices alongside the roasted vegetables, garnished with fresh rosemary.

Baked Salmon With Lemon And Dill

Ingredients:

- 1 lemon, thinly sliced
- 2 tablespoons fresh dill, chopped
- 2 salmon fillets
- 2 tablespoons olive oil
- Salt and pepper to taste

Directions:
1. Preheat your oven to 375°F (190°C).
2. Place the salmon fillets on a baking sheet lined with parchment paper.
3. Drizzle olive oil over the salmon and season with salt and pepper.
4. Place lemon slices on top of the salmon fillets and sprinkle fresh dill over them.

5. Wrap the salmon in parchment paper and aluminum foil, creating a packet.
6. Bake in the preheated oven for 15-20 minutes, or until the salmon flakes easily with a fork.
7. Unwrap the salmon and serve it hot, garnished with extra dill and lemon slices.

Lemon Garlic Grilled Shrimp

Ingredients:

- Zest and juice of 1 lemon
- 2 tablespoons olive oil
- Salt and pepper to taste
- 1 lb large shrimp, peeled and deveined
- 2 cloves garlic, minced
- Fresh parsley for garnish (optional)

Directions:

1. In a bowl, combine minced garlic, lemon zest, lemon juice, olive oil, salt, and pepper to create the marinade.
2. Toss the shrimp in the marinade and let them marinate for 15-20 minutes.
3. Preheat your grill to medium-high heat.

4. Thread the marinated shrimp onto skewers.
5. Grill the shrimp for 2-3 minutes per side, or until they turn pink and slightly charred.
6. Serve the Lemon Garlic Grilled Shrimp hot, garnished with fresh parsley if desired.

Bacon, Avocado And Jack Cheese Omelet With Salsa

Ingredients:

- 6 slices bacon, cooked, crumbled
- 2 cups Monterey Jack cheese, shredded
- 2 ounces water
- 8 large eggs
- 2 tablespoons butter, unsalted

For salsa:

- 2 tablespoons fresh lime juice
- 2 tablespoons fresh cilantro, chopped
- Salt to taste
- 1 large ripe tomato, chopped

- 1 jalapeño pepper, finely chopped
- 1 avocado, peeled, pitted, chopped
- 6 medium spring onions, finely chopped
- Pepper powder to taste

Directions:
1. To make salsa: Mix together all the Ingredients: of the salsa and set aside.
2. Whisk together eggs, water, salt and pepper.
3. Place a nonstick skillet over medium heat. Add 1/2-tablespoon butter. When the butter melts, add 1/4 of the egg mixture. Lightly swirl the pan so that the egg spreads.
4. Cook until nearly set. Sprinkle 1/4 each of bacon, avocado and cheese over one half of the omelet.
5. Fold the other half over it. Remove on to a plate and serve.

6. Repeat steps 3 and 4 with the remaining egg mixture and filling.

Scrambled Eggs

Ingredients:

- Pepper powder to taste
- 1 teaspoon fresh parsley, chopped
- 1/2 teaspoon fresh tarragon, chopped
- 3 large eggs
- 1 tablespoon heavy cream
- Salt to taste
- 1/2 tablespoon unsalted butter

Directions:
1. Whisk together eggs, cream, salt, pepper, tarragon, and parsley.
2. Place a nonstick skillet over medium heat. Add butter.

3. When the butter melts, add the egg mixture. Cook for a minute. Then scramble it with a wooden spoon.
4. When the eggs are soft and creamy, remove from heat and serve immediately.

Beef Huevos Rancheros

Ingredients:

- 1/2 teaspoon garlic powder
- 1/2 teaspoon ground cumin
- Salt to taste
- Pepper to taste
- 1/2 teaspoon dried oregano
- 3/4 cup cheddar cheese, shredded
- 2-3 tablespoons fresh cilantro, chopped
- 6 large eggs
- 9 ounces lean ground beef
- 6 slices Canadian bacon
- 3/4 cup canned green chili pepper

- 1 1/2 teaspoons chili powder

- Cooking spray

Directions:
1. Place a skillet over medium heat. Spray with cooking spray. Add beef and cook until brown.
2. Add chilies, garlic powder, chili powder, cumin, oregano, salt and pepper and cook for another 5-7 minutes.
3. Place the bacon slices on top of the beef and remove from heat.
4. Place a skillet over medium heat. Spray with cooking spray. Add eggs, cook until lightly set and scramble it.
5. To serve: Place a slice of bacon on each plate. Divide the beef mixture into 6 portions and place over the bacon.
6. Divide the scrambled eggs and place over the beef.

7. Sprinkle cheese and cilantro and serve.

2-Step Chia Yogurt

Ingredients:

- 1 tbsp. Almonds, unsalted, sliced

- ¼ tsp. Almond extract

- ½ tsp. Turmeric spice

- ½ Cup or 5.3 oz. Greek yogurt, plain, whole milk

- ½ tbsp. Chia seeds

- 1 pinch ground cinnamon

Directions:

1. Place all ingredients into container of choice, stirring well to combine.
2. Enjoy immediately or store in the refrigerator overnight, if you would prefer to allow the

chia seeds to absorb the yogurt and expand overnight.

Spanish Braised Chicken In Creamy Almond Sauce

Ingredients:

- 2 Tbsp. Sundried tomatoes, chopped
- 1 tsp. Smoked paprika
- 1/2 yellow bell pepper, deseeded and diced
- 1 serrano or jalapeno pepper, deseeded and diced
- 1/2 red bell pepper, deseeded and diced
- 2 sprigs fresh thyme
- 1 cup chicken broth or water
- 1/3 cup almonds, chopped
- 1/4 cup pitted Spanish manzanilla olives (or other green olives), sliced

- 4 Tbsp. Flat leaf parsley, chopped and divided
- 2 Tbsp. Olive oil
- 1 lb. Boneless skinless chicken thighs
- 2 Tbsp. Unsalted butter
- 1 medium onion, chopped
- 3 cloves garlic, minced
- 1 lemon, juiced and zested

Directions:
1. Heat olive oil in a large skillet over medium-high heat.
2. Pat chicken thighs dry then season with salt and pepper to taste. Add to pan and cook 4 to 6 minutes per side, until cooked through. Transfer to a plate and set aside.

3. Add onions to the skillet and cook over medium heat for 3 to 5 minutes, or until translucent.
4. Stir in garlic, sundried tomatoes, paprika, peppers and thyme. Cook, stirring occasionally, for 4 to 5 minutes until the vegetables are tender.
5. Add chicken thighs and broth to the skillet and bring to a boil. Reduce the heat to medium-low and cook 12 to 15 minutes, stirring occasionally.
6. Add almonds, olives, 3 Tablespoons of parsley, lemon zest and lemon juice. Reduce heat to low and simmer for 6 to 8 minutes longer.
7. Garnish with remaining parsley before serving.

H Omemade Calzone With Cauliflower Crust

Ingredients:

- ¼ tsp. garlic powder
- 2 tsp. black pepper
- ¼ cup bell peppers, diced
- ¼ cup tomatoes, diced
- 1.5 oz. skinless chicken breast strips
- ¼ cup ricotta cheddar, whole milk
- 2 cups cauliflower (about ½ of a medium-sized head), riced
- 1 large egg
- ¼ cup mozzarella cheddar, shredded
- ½ tsp. Oregano

- 4 basil leaves, chopped

Directions:
1. Preheat the oven to 400° F and line a baking sheet with parchment paper.
2. Chop cauliflower into florets and add to a food processor (fitted with an S.blade) or blender and pulse until a rice-like surface is accomplished. You can also purchase pre-riced cauliflower from the supermarket.
3. Transfer cauliflower to a microwave-safe bowl and microwave on high for about 2 to 3 minutes or until cauliflower is relaxed. Let cool.
4. When the cauliflower is cool enough to handle , utilize a perfect drying towel, paper towel or cheddar cloth and channel it (over the sink) of any excess water.
5. Transfer cauliflower to a spotless bowl and mix in the egg, two tablespoons of shredded

mozzarella cheese, oregano, black pepper and garlic powder. Mix it until combined.
6. Divide the cauliflower combination in half and structure into two circular shapes on the arranged baking sheet. Prepare for around 15 to 20 minutes or until it is golden brown.
7. When the cauliflower calzone crusts are cooked , fill them equally with the diced bell peppers, tomatoes and basil.
8. Sprinkle each calzone with one tablespoon of mozzarella cheddar. Crease each outside layer in half to cover the filling and make the calzone.
9. Place calzones back in the oven and bake them for an extra 7-10 minutes or until the cheese is dissolved and enjoy!

Chocolate Peanut Butter Mug Muffins

Ingredients:

- 2 Tbsp. creamy natural peanut butter, unsalted and unsweetened
- 1 ½ Tbsp. unsalted butter or ghee
- 1 Tbsp. ground flaxseeds
- 1 scoop (about 2 Tbsp.) keto well disposed vanilla protein powder
- ¼ tsp. baking powder
- 2 ½ Tbsp. fullfat sour cream or plain whole-milk Greek yogurt
- 1 enormous egg
- 2 tsp. powdered erythritol sweetener
- 2 Tbsp. sugar-free chocolate chips

Directions:

1. Split all ingredients except for the chocolate chips between two large mugs. Whisk with a fork until well combined.
2. Stir in the chocolate chips.
3. Cook in the microwave for about 1 to 1 ½ minutes, until the combination is set in the center.

Southern Stuffed Eggs

Ingredients:

- 1/5 tsp. pepper
- 5 slices bacon, crisply fried and finely crumbled
- 1/2 C. mayonnaise or salad dressing
- 1/2 to 1 tsp. white vinegar
- 12 hardboiled eggs
- 1/2 tsp. salt
- 1 tsp. dry mustard
- Paprika

Directions:

1. Cut peeled eggs in half lengthwise. Take out yolks and mash with fork.

2. Mix in salt, mustard, pepper, bacon, mayonnaise and vinegar.
3. Fill egg whites with yolk mixture. Sprinkle with paprika. Keep covered in refrigerator. 1/4 cup finely chopped sweet pickles may be substituted for bacon for a different flavor.

Trattoria Frittata

Ingredients:

- 8 eggs
- 1/2 cup (4 oz.) part?skim ricotta cheese
- 1 teaspoon garlic powder
- 1 small tomato, thinly sliced
- 8 ounces bulk Italian sausage
- 1 cup chopped green pepper
- 1 teaspoon fennel seed
- 1/4 cup (1 oz.) shredded part skim mozzarella cheese

Directions:

1. In 10inch omelet pan or skillet with ovenproof handle+ over medium heat, cook sausage,

green pepper and fennel seed, stirring to break sausage apart, until sausage is browned, about 3 to 5 minutes. Drain well. Return to pan.
2. In medium bowl, beat together eggs, ricotta cheese and garlic powder until blended. Pour into pan over sausage mixture. Cover.
3. Cook over medium heat until eggs are almost set, about 8 to 10 minutes. Top with tomato slices. Sprinkle with mozzarella cheese.
4. Broil about 6 inches from heat until cheese is melted, about 1 to 2 minutes.
5. Cut into wedge and serve from pan or slide from pan onto serving platter.

Lentil Soup

Ingredients:

- 2 stalks celery, diced
- 3 1/2 cups crushed tomatoes
- 1 1/2 cups lentils ? soaked, rinsed and drained
- 1/2 teaspoon salt
- 1/2 teaspoon ground black pepper
- 3/4 cup white wine
- 2 bay leaves
- 7 cups chicken stock
- 1 sprig fresh parsley, chopped
- 1/2 teaspoon paprika
- 2 tablespoons olive oil
- 2 large onions, cubed
- 1 teaspoon minced garlic

- 3 carrots, diced

- 1/2 cup grated Parmesan cheese

Directions:

1. In a large stockpot, saute the onions in oil until they are glossy.
2. Stir in garlic, paprika, celery, carrots, and saute for 10 minutes.
3. Once the vegetables have sauteed for 10 minutes stir in tomatoes, chicken stock, lentils, bay leaves, salt, and pepper.
4. Stir well, then add the wine and bring the mixture to a boil. Slowly reduce the heat and cook for 1 hour on low to medium heat; or until the lentils are tender.
5. Sprinkle the soup with parsley and Parmesan before serving.

Rare Roast Beef Salad With Mustard Mayonnaise
From Amy Kanarios

Ingredients:

Dressing:

- 2 tablespoons finely chopped chives

- 1 tablespoon drained tiny capers

- 1 tablespoon finely chopped sun-dried bell pepper (capsicum)

- 1/3 cup (3 1/2 fl oz/100 ml) olive oil

- 1/4 cup (2 fl oz/60 ml) lemon juice

- Salt and freshly ground black pepper

- Combine all of the dressing Ingredients: in a small bowl. Whisk together until well blended.

Mustard mayonnaise:

- 2 teaspoons Worcestershire sauce
- A few drops of Tabasco sauce
- 1/4 cup (2 fl oz/60 ml) mayonnaise
- 1 tablespoon Dijon mustard
- Combine all the mayonnaise ingredients in a small bowl. Stir until well blended.

Salad:

- 3 lbs (1.5 kg) rare roast beef, sliced - allow 2 large slices per person
- 6 oz (185 g) cherry tomatoes, halved
- 1 head (3 1/2 oz/100 g) radicchio, washed and torn
- 1 bunch (3 1/2 oz/100g) lamb's lettuce, washed and torn
- 1 jar (8 oz/250 g) artichoke hearts, halved

- 1/3 cup (2 1/2 oz/75 g) tiny cornichons (tiny gherkins or dill pickles)

Directions:
1. Divide the remaining ingredients among 6 serving plates.
2. Spoon the dressing over and place a tablespoon of mayonnaise in the center of each salad.

Broccoli, Bacon, And Cheese Quiche

Ingredients:

- ½ teaspoon salt
- 2 pounds frozen broccoli florets, thawed
- 6 ounces bacon, cooked and crumbled
- ¾ cup shredded medium Cheddar cheese, divided
- 8 large eggs
- 2 cups reduced-fat 2% milk
- ½ cup grated Parmesan cheese

Directions:
1. Coat a slow cooker generously with cooking spray.
2. In a medium bowl, whisk together the eggs, milk, Parmesan, and salt.

3. Add the broccoli, bacon, and half the Cheddar cheese to the slow cooker. Pour in the egg mixture. Top with the remaining Cheddar cheese.
4. Cook on low for 6 to 8 hours or on high for 3 to 4 hours, or until the eggs are set.

Granola

Ingredients:

- ½ cup dried berries
- ¼ cup chia seeds
- 1 teaspoon cinnamon
- ½ teaspoon salt
- ¼ teaspoon nutmeg
- ¼ cup coconut oil
- 2½ cups almonds
- ¼ cup unsweetened coconut flakes
- 1 teaspoon vanilla

Directions:

1. Coat the sides of a slow cooker generously with cooking spray.

2. Add the almonds, coconut flakes, dried berries, chia seeds, cinnamon, salt, and nutmeg to the slow cooker.
3. In a medium bowl, melt the coconut oil. Whisk in the vanilla.
4. Pour the mixture into the slow cooker, stirring to make sure all the ingredients are moistened.
5. Lay a small towel or 2 paper towels in between the slow cooker and the lid to create a barrier.
6. This will prevent the condensation from dripping on the granola while it cooks. It's important to catch the condensation or you will end up with soggy granola.
7. Cook mixture on low for 6 hours or on high for 3 hours. Transfer the granola to a baking sheet to cool.

Cauliflower Mac And Cheese

Ingredients:

- 2 medium heads cauliflower, cut into small florets
- 1 small onion, diced
- 3 cups Cheese Sauce

Directions:
1. Coat a slow cooker generously with cooking spray.
2. Add the cauliflower and onion to the slow cooker.
3. Pour the cheese sauce over the top.
4. Cook on low for 4 to 6 hours or on high for 2 to 3 hours, or until the cauliflower is tender.

Breakfast Mix

Ingredients:

- 1 cup rice cereal
- ¼ cup cocoa cereal
- 1 cup corn cereal
- ¼ cup rice cakes

Directions:
1. In a bowl combine all Ingredients: together
2. Serve with milk

Sausage Breakfast Sandwich

Ingredients:

- 1 muffin
- 1 turkey sausage patty
- ¼ cup egg substitute
- 1 tablespoon cheddar cheese

Directions:

1. In a skillet pour egg and cook on low heat
2. Place turkey sausage patty in a pan and cook for 4-5 minutes per side
3. On a toasted muffin place the cooked egg, top with a sausage patty and cheddar cheese
4. Serve when ready

Strawberry Yogurt

Ingredients:

- 1 cup plain low-fat Greek yoghurt
- 1 cup fresh raspberries or strawberries your choice
- 3 cups unsweetened coconut milk
- 4 large scoops of vanilla protein shake (low carbs of course)
- 2 Tbsp. chia seeds
- Handful of unsweetened coconut flakes as topping

Directions:

1. In a large mixing bowl, mix all the Ingredients:, except the fruits.

2. You could use the blender and blend for just a few seconds, so you can still have some great thickness and consistency. I prefer to simply use a wooden spoon and mix for several minutes.
3. Pour into 4 individual bowls or cups and divide the fruits as toppings and the coconut flakes.

Delicious Baked Garlic Salmon Filets

Ingredients:

- 1 Tbsp. cilantro paste

- ½ cup chopped sundried tomatoes

- 1 cup hot water

- 1 tbsp.., miso pasta

- 1 Tbsp. balsamic vinegar

- 4 salmon filets

- 2 Tbsp. avocado oil

- 2 Tbsp. minced fresh garlic

- Salt, black pepper

- Fresh minced parsley to decorate

Directions:

1. Preheat the oven to 350 degrees F.
2. Grease a large baking dish and place the filets skin down.
3. In a medium mixing bowl, combine the miso pasta and the hot water, set aside for now.
4. In a different bowl, combine the vinegar, garlic, avocado oil, the cilantro paste (you can purchase any store in produce section)
5. Use a brush to brush off each salmon filets with the oily mixture.
6. Place the salmon I the oven for 10 minutes.
7. Remove from the oven and pour the miso pasta mixture on top and sprinkle the chopped sundried tomatoes as well.
8. Place in the oven for another 10-12 minutes. When done serve with fresh parsley on top.

Egg Muffins

Ingredients:

- ½ diced red bell pepper
- Salt, black pepper
- ½ tsp. garlic powder
- ½ tsp. onion powder
- 8 large eggs
- ½ cup skim milk
- 1 cup low fat ricotta cheese
- ½ diced green bell pepper
- 1 tbsp. chili powder

Directions:
1. Preheat the oven to 350 degrees F.
2. Grease a muffin tin and set aside.

3. In a large mixing bowl, combine the eggs, milks, ricotta cheese and all seasonings.
4. In a medium pan, heat the oil and cook for 5-6 minutes the bell peppers.
5. Add to the first mixture and then combine.
6. Pour into the muffin holes and bake for about 45 minutes. Serve as soon as done and cooled down.

Grilled Chicken Caesar Salad Wrap

Ingredients:

- 1/4 cup Caesar dressing
- 1/4 cup grated Parmesan cheese
- 2 cups romaine lettuce, chopped
- 2-3 oz grilled chicken breast, sliced
- 1 whole wheat wrap

Directions:

1. Spread Caesar dressing on the whole wheat wrap.
2. Layer grilled chicken breast, grated Parmesan cheese, and romaine lettuce on top of the Caesar dressing.
3. Roll up the wrap and serve.

Veggie Hummus Wrap

Ingredients:

- 1/4 cup mixed veggies (such as bell peppers, cucumbers, and carrots), diced
- 2 tbsp crumbled feta cheese
- 1 whole wheat wrap
- 1/4 cup hummus
- Salt and pepper to taste

Directions:

1. Spread hummus on the whole wheat wrap.
2. Add mixed veggies and crumbled feta cheese on top of the hummus.
3. Season with salt and pepper to taste.
4. Roll up the wrap and serve.

Homemade Protein Bars

Ingredients:

- 1/4 cup honey
- 1/4 cup protein powder
- 1/4 cup chopped nuts (optional)
- 1 cup rolled oats
- 1/2 cup peanut butter
- 1/4 cup dried fruit (optional)

Directions:

1. In a large mixing bowl, combine rolled oats, protein powder, and chopped nuts (if using).
2. In a separate bowl, mix together peanut butter and honey until smooth.

3. Add peanut butter and honey mixture to the dry Ingredients: and stir until everything is well combined.
4. Fold in dried fruit (if using).
5. Transfer mixture to a lined 8x8-inch baking dish and press down firmly.
6. Refrigerate for at least 1 hour or until the mixture is firm.
7. Cut into bars and enjoy.

Roasted Red Pepper Dip

Ingredients:

- 1/4 cup tahini
- 2 garlic cloves, minced
- 2 tbsp lemon juice
- 1 tbsp olive oil
- 2 red bell peppers
- 1/4 cup plain Greek yogurt
- 1/4 tsp salt

Directions:

1. Preheat the oven to 400°F.
2. Cut the red bell peppers into quarters and remove the seeds and stem.

3. Place the peppers on a baking sheet and roast for 20-25 minutes, or until the skin is blistered and blackened.
4. Remove the peppers from the oven and place them in a bowl. Cover the bowl with plastic wrap and let the peppers steam for 10-15 minutes.
5. Once the peppers have cooled, remove the skin and place the flesh in a food processor.
6. Add the Greek yogurt, tahini, garlic, lemon juice, olive oil, and salt to the food processor and blend until smooth.
7. Transfer the dip to a bowl and serve with raw vegetables like carrot sticks, celery, or cucumber.

Chicken With Mushroom And Leeks

Ingredients:

- 1 leek, white part only, sliced

- 500ml (2 cups) Massel chicken style liquid stock

- 2 garlic cloves, crushed

- 200g Swiss brown mushrooms, cleaned, sliced

- 5 fresh thyme sprigs

- 1 tbsp Dijon mustard

- 1 tbsp crème fraîche

- Blanched broccolini or green beans, to serve

- 4 small chicken breasts

- 2 tsp olive oil

- 25g dried porcini mushrooms

- 180ml (3/4 cup) warm water
- 2 green shallots, sliced
- Fresh baby parsley leaves, to serve

Directions:

1. Place chicken on a plate and drizzle with 1 tsp of oil. Toss to coat. Season well.
2. Place dried porcini mushrooms in a bowl and cover with warm water. Set aside for 10 minutes to soak.
3. Drain, reserving soaking liquid. Roughly chop rehydrated porcini and set aside.
4. Heat a large heavy-based frying pan over high heat.
5. Cook chicken for 3 minutes or until golden on 1 side.
6. Turn and cook for 3 minutes or until almost cooked through. Transfer to a clean plate.
7. Reduce heat to medium and add remaining oil. Cook shallot and leek, stirring, for 5

minutes or until golden and caramelized. Add stock, garlic, porcini and soaking liquid, mushroom, thyme and mustard.
8. Stir and bring to a simmer. Return chicken to the pan. Cook for 5 minutes. Stir in crème fraîche.
9. Simmer for a further 3-5 minutes or until sauce has reduced and thickened.
10. Slice chicken and serve with mushroom sauce and broccolini or green beans.
11. Top with baby parsley leaves to serve.

Lime And Potato Coconut Curry With Fish

Ingredients:

- 3 teaspoons finely grated fresh turmeric
- 275ml salt-reduced vegetable stock
- 250ml (1 cup) light coconut milk
- 2 slender eggplants, sliced
- 2 zucchini, sliced into rounds
- 600g thick white fish (such as ling), cut into 3cm pieces
- 2 tsp fish sauce
- 1 lime, rind finely grated, juiced, plus extra wedges, to serve
- 450g sweet potato, peeled, cut into 2cm pieces

- 350g kipfler potatoes, peeled, cut into 2cm pieces

- 1 large onion, chopped

- 2 garlic cloves, crushed

- 1 tbsp finely grated fresh ginger

- Fresh Thai basil leaves, to serve

Directions:
1. Spray a large non-stick frying pan with oil.
2. Place over medium-high heat.
3. Add sweet potato, potato and onion. Cook, stirring, for 1-2 minutes.
4. Add the garlic, ginger and turmeric.
5. Season well and stir to coat.
6. Add stock and coconut milk. Bring almost to the boil. Reduce heat. Simmer, covered, for 10 minutes. Uncover and simmer for 5 minutes.
7. Add eggplant and zucchini. Simmer, covered, for 10 minutes or until eggplant is tender.

8. Add fish, fish sauce, lime rind and juice. Simmer, covered, for 5 minutes or until fish is cooked through.
9. Divide curry among serving bowls.
10. Top with basil.
11. Serve with extra lime.

Baked Chicken With Sweet Potato

Ingredients:

- 2 tablespoons olive oil
- 1 teaspoon paprika
- 1 teaspoon garlic powder
- ½ teaspoon dried thyme
- 4 bone-in chicken thighs
- 2 medium sweet potatoes
- Salt and pepper, to taste

Directions:
1. Preheat your oven to 425°F (220°C).
2. Wash and peel the sweet potatoes.
3. Cut them into 1-inch cubes and set aside.
4. In a small bowl, mix together the paprika, garlic powder, dried thyme, salt, and pepper.

5. Pat dry the chicken thighs with a paper towel.
6. Place them on a baking sheet lined with parchment paper.
7. Drizzle olive oil over the chicken thighs and rub them with the spice mixture, ensuring they are evenly coated.
8. In a separate bowl, toss the sweet potato cubes with olive oil, salt, and pepper.
9. Place the seasoned sweet potato cubes around the chicken thighs on the baking sheet.
10. Bake in the preheated oven for about 30-35 minutes or until the chicken reaches an internal temperature of 165°F (74°C) and the sweet potatoes are tender.
11. You can flip the chicken thighs halfway through for even cooking.
12. Remove from the oven and let the chicken rest for a few minutes before serving.

Mediterranean Chickpea Salad:

Ingredients:

- 1/2 red onion, finely chopped
- 1/4 cup of fresh parsley, chopped
- 1/4 cup of feta cheese (optional)
- 2mtablespoons of olive oil
- 1 tablespoons of lemon juice
- 1 teaspoon of dried oregano
- 1 can (15 oz) of chickpeas, drained and rinsed
- 1 cucumber, diced
- 1 cup of cherry tomatoes, halved
- Salt and pepper to your taste

Directions:

1. In a large bowl, mix together chickpeas, diced cucumber, halved cherry tomatoes,

finely chopped red onion, and freshly chopped parsley.
2. In a separate small bowl, whisk together olive oil, lemon juice, dried oregano, salt, and pepper to create the dressing.
3. Pour the dressing over the salad and toss everything together until well combined.
4. If desired, you can sprinkle crumbled feta cheese on top for an extra burst of flavor.
5. Refrigerate the salad for approximately 30 minutes before serving. It offers a refreshing and low-glycemic index meal option.

Spinach And Mozzarella Frittata

Ingredients:

- 1/4 cup of diced onion
- 1/2 tablespoon of extra virgin olive oil
- 1/3 cup of grated Parmesan & Romano cheese blend
- 6 large Eggland's Best eggs
- 2 cups of fresh baby spinach
- 2/3 cup of fresh mozzarella cheese, cubed

Directions:
1. Preheat your oven to 400 degrees F.
2. Spray an oven-safe skillet with non-stick cooking spray and heat it over medium-high heat.

3. Add the olive oil to the pan, and when it's hot, sauté the onion.
4. As the onion begins to brown, introduce the spinach and continue cooking until the spinach wilts. Remove from heat and let it cool.
5. In a large bowl, whisk together the eggs, salt, pepper, Parmesan and Romano cheeses.
6. Pour the egg mixture over the vegetables in the skillet and sprinkle bite-sized pieces of fresh mozzarella cheese on top.
7. Bake in the oven for 25 minutes or until the eggs have set.

Peanut Butter And Jelly Cookies

Ingredients:

- 75g golden caster sugar

- 1 medium egg

- 1 tsp vanilla extract

- 180g plain flour

- 2 tbsp chopped peanuts

- ½ tsp bicarbonate of soda

- 70g softened butter

- 50g peanut butter

- 75g light brown sugar

- 10 heaped tsp raspberry jam

Directions:

1. Preheat your oven to 180°C (160°C fan/gas 4) and line two baking sheets with parchment paper.
2. Cream together the softened butter, peanut butter, and both sugars until the mixture becomes very light and fluffy. Then, mix in the egg and vanilla extract.
3. Once combined, fold in the plain flour, chopped peanuts, bicarbonate of soda, and ¼ tsp of salt.
4. Use a spoon to scoop out 10 large tablespoons of the mixture onto the prepared trays, leaving enough space between each for spreading.
5. Create a thumbprint in the center of each cookie and fill it with 1 heaped teaspoon of raspberry jam (homemade jam is an option).
6. Bake in the oven for 10-12 minutes or until the edges become firm but the centers are still soft they will firm up a bit as they cool.

7. Allow them to cool on the tray for a few minutes before enjoying them warm, or transfer them to a wire rack to cool completely.

Vegetable And Chickpea Curry

Ingredients:

- 1 can (14 oz) diced tomatoes
- 1 can (14 oz) coconut milk
- 2 tablespoons curry powder
- 1 tablespoon olive oil
- Salt and pepper to taste
- Fresh cilantro for garnish (optional)
- 2 cups mixed vegetables (e.g., carrots, bell peppers, peas)
- 1 can (15 oz) chickpeas, drained and rinsed
- 1 onion, finely chopped
- 2 cloves garlic, minced

- Cooked rice or naan bread for serving

Directions:
1. In a large skillet, heat olive oil over medium heat.
2. Add finely chopped onion and minced garlic. Sauté until fragrant and translucent.
3. Stir in curry powder and cook for an additional minute.
4. Add mixed vegetables, chickpeas, diced tomatoes (with juice), and coconut milk to the skillet.
5. Season with salt and pepper, and simmer for 15-20 minutes, or until the vegetables are tender and the sauce thickens.
6. Serve the Vegetable and Chickpea Curry over cooked rice or with naan bread, garnished with fresh cilantro if desired.

Cauliflower And Broccoli Soup

Ingredients:

- 2 cloves garlic, minced
- 4 cups vegetable broth
- 1 cup milk (or dairy-free alternative)
- 2 tablespoons olive oil
- Salt and pepper to taste
- 1 head cauliflower, chopped into florets
- 1 head broccoli, chopped into florets
- 1 onion, chopped
- Fresh chives for garnish (optional)

Directions:

1. In a large pot, heat olive oil over medium heat.

2. Add chopped onions and minced garlic. Sauté until the onions are translucent.
3. Add cauliflower and broccoli florets to the pot.
4. Pour in vegetable broth and bring to a boil. Reduce heat and simmer for 20-25 minutes until the vegetables are tender.
5. Use an immersion blender or a regular blender to puree the soup until smooth.
6. Return the pureed soup to the pot and stir in milk.
7. Season with salt and pepper to taste.
8. Serve the Cauliflower and Broccoli Soup hot, garnished with fresh chives if desired.

Turkey And Vegetable Skewers

Ingredients:

- 2 tablespoons olive oil

- Juice of 1 lemon

- 2 cloves garlic, minced

- 1 teaspoon paprika

- Salt and pepper to taste

- 1 lb turkey breast, cut into cubes

- 2 bell peppers (various colors), cut into chunks

- 1 red onion, cut into chunks

- 1 zucchini, sliced

- Wooden skewers, soaked in water

Directions:

1. In a bowl, combine olive oil, lemon juice, minced garlic, paprika, salt, and pepper to create the marinade.
2. Thread turkey pieces, bell pepper chunks, red onion chunks, and zucchini slices onto wooden skewers, alternating between turkey and vegetables.
3. Brush the skewers with the marinade.
4. Preheat your grill to medium-high heat.
5. Grill the skewers for 10-12 minutes, turning occasionally, until the turkey is cooked through and the vegetables are tender and slightly charred.
6. Serve the Turkey and Vegetable Skewers hot, accompanied by your favorite side dishes.

Fried Eggs And Vegetables

Ingredients:

- 1/2 cup broccoli florets, chopped into small pieces
- 1 cup spinach, thinly sliced
- Salt to taste
- Pepper to taste
- 1/4 teaspoon chili powder
- 4 eggs, beaten
- 1 tablespoon extra virgin olive oil
- 1/2 cup cauliflower florets, chopped into small pieces
- 1/2 teaspoon dried oregano

Directions:

1. Place a nonstick skillet over medium high heat. Add oil. When the oil is heated, add cauliflower and broccoli and sauté for 3-4 minutes.
2. Add eggs, salt, pepper, chili powder and oregano and stir.
3. Add spinach and stir until the eggs are cooked.
4. Serve hot.

Cheesy Tuna Casserole

Ingredients:

- 3 tablespoons onion, finely chopped
- 3 tablespoons butter
- 3/4 cup chicken broth
- 1 cup heavy cream or more if required
- Salt to taste
- Pepper powder to taste
- Xanthan gum (optional)
- 3 cans (6 ounce each) tuna, drained
- 24 ounces frozen chopped French green beans, cooked according to Directions: on the package
- 5 ounces fresh mushrooms, chopped,

- 2 stalks celery, finely chopped

- 8 ounces cheddar cheese, shredded

Directions:
1. Place a skillet over medium heat. Add butter. When butter melts, add onions and sauté for a couple of minutes. Add mushrooms and celery and sauté until light brown.
2. Add broth and boil until the broth reduces in quantity by half. Reduce heat and simmer until thick. Stir frequently.
3. Add salt, pepper, tuna, beans and the sautéed mushrooms to a casserole dish.
4. Top with cheese. Bake in a preheated oven at 325° F until the cheese is melted and bubbling.

Baby Spinach Omelet

Ingredients:

- 1/2 teaspoon onion powder
- 1/4 teaspoon ground nutmeg
- Salt to taste
- Pepper powder to taste
- 4 eggs, whisked well
- 2 cups baby spinach, torn
- 3 tablespoons parmesan, grated
- Cooking spray

Directions:

1. Add eggs, spinach, and cheese, nutmeg, salt, pepper and onion powder to a bowl and mix well.

2. Place a nonstick pan over medium heat. Spray with cooking spray.
3. Pour the egg mixture and cook until almost set and the underside is golden brown.
4. Flip sides and cook the other side too.
5. Serve hot.

1-Minute Chocolate Ricotta Mousse

Ingredients:

- 1 tbsp. Unsweetened vanilla almond milk
- 1 tbsp. Unsweetened cocoa powder
- 2-3 drops stevia
- ½ Cup part-skim ricotta cheese
- 1 tsp. Cacao nibs

Directions:

1. In a small blender or food processor whip together ricotta cheese, almond milk, cocoa powder and stevia until smooth. Top with cacao nibs and serve.

No-Bake Strawberry Cheesecake Bliss Balls

Ingredients:

- 1 tsp. vanilla extract
- 2 Tbsp. erythritol-based sweetener (granulated)
- 1/8 tsp. salt
- 1 cup raw cashews
- 2 Tbsp. coconut oil
- 1/4 cup freeze-dried strawberries

Directions:

1. Pulse cashews, coconut oil, vanilla extract, erythritol and salt in a food processor until a dough forms.
2. Add berries and pulse again until just combined.

3. Divide dough into 8 pieces, then roll between the palms of your hands to form balls.
4. Store in the refrigerator for up to 1 week.

Instant Pot Keto Tuscan Soup

Ingredients:

- ½ cup sun-dried tomatoes, drained

- Salt and black pepper, to taste

- 6 cups chicken broth, low sodium

- 1 bunch kale, leaves stripped from stems and chopped

- ¾ cup heavy cream

- ¼ cup grated parmesan

- 1 lb. Italian chicken sausage (hot or mild), casings removed

- 1 large onion, chopped

- 3 cloves garlic, minced

- 1 tsp. dried oregano

- Fresh parsley, chopped (optional)

Directions:
1. Set a 6-quart Instant Pot to sauté mode. Add the chicken sausage (casings removed) and break it up with a spoon while cooking. Continue cooking until the sausage is lightly browned, about 3-5 minutes.
2. Add in the garlic, onion and oregano. Stir constantly until the onions become translucent, about 2-3 minutes.
3. Add in the chicken broth and sun-dried tomatoes. Stir to combine. Season with pepper.
4. Set the Instant to Pot to Manual High Pressure for 5 minutes. When finished cooking, do a quick-release.
5. Select sauté mode and add in the kale. Stir until wilted, about 1-2 minutes.
6. Stir in the heavy cream and continue cooking until heated through, about 1 minute. Season

with salt and pepper to taste, as needed. Remove from the heat.
7. Garnish with fresh grated parmesan and parsley and serve immediately.

Lobster Salad In Endive Guacamole Dip Or Salad Dressing

Ingredients:

- 2 tbsp. Mayonnaise
- Salt and pepper to taste
- Dash of tabasco sauce
- Dash of worcestershire sauce
- Very finely chopped jalapenos peppers to taste
- 3 ripe avocados
- 3 tbsp. Lemon juice
- 1 small onion very fine chopped
- 1 tsp. Garlic powder
- 1 chopped ripe tomato

Directions:

1. Placed peeled and cut avocados in a medium bowl and on low speed blend with mixer.
2. Add remaining ingredients, adding jalapenos to suit your taste and blend until mixture is thoroughly blended together but not soupy.
3. Chill and serve on lettuce as salad or with chips as dip. Place avocado pits in mixture while being stored in refrigerator to keep mixture.

Lentil Soup

Ingredients:

- 3 1/2 cups crushed tomatoes

- 1 1/2 cups lentils ? soaked, rinsed and drained

- 1/2 teaspoon salt

- 1/2 teaspoon ground black pepper

- 3/4 cup white wine

- 2 bay leaves

- 7 cups chicken stock

- 1 sprig fresh parsley, chopped

- 1/2 teaspoon paprika

- 2 tablespoons olive oil

- 2 large onions, cubed

- 1 teaspoon minced garlic

- 3 carrots, diced

- 2 stalks celery, diced

- 1/2 cup grated Parmesan cheese

Directions:

1. In a large stockpot, saute the onions in oil until they are glossy. Stir in garlic, paprika, celery, carrots, and saute for 10 minutes.
2. Once the vegetables have sauteed for 10 minutes stir in tomatoes, chicken stock, lentils, bay leaves, salt, and pepper.
3. Stir well, then add the wine and bring the mixture to a boil. Slowly reduce the heat and cook for 1 hour on low to medium heat; or until the lentils are tender.
4. Sprinkle the soup with parsley and Parmesan before serving.

Rare Roast Beef Salad With Mustard Mayonnaise
From Amy Kanarios

Ingredients:

Dressing:

- 2 tablespoons finely chopped chives

- 1 tablespoon drained tiny capers

- 1 tablespoon finely chopped sun-dried bell pepper (capsicum)

- 1/3 cup (3 1/2 fl oz/100 ml) olive oil

- 1/4 cup (2 fl oz/60 ml) lemon juice

- Salt and freshly ground black pepper

- Combine all of the dressing Ingredients: in a small bowl. Whisk together until well blended.

Mustard mayonnaise:

- 1/4 cup (2 fl oz/60 ml) mayonnaise

- 1 tablespoon Dijon mustard

- 2 teaspoons Worcestershire sauce

- A few drops of Tabasco sauce

- Combine all the mayonnaise ingredients in a small bowl. Stir until well blended.

Salad:

- 1 bunch (3 1/2 oz/100g) lamb's lettuce, washed and torn

- 1 jar (8 oz/250 g) artichoke hearts, halved

- 1/3 cup (2 1/2 oz/75 g) tiny cornichons (tiny gherkins or dill pickles)

- 3 lbs (1.5 kg) rare roast beef, sliced - allow 2 large slices per person

- 6 oz (185 g) cherry tomatoes, halved

- 1 head (3 1/2 oz/100 g) radicchio, washed and torn

Directions:
1. Divide the remaining ingredients among 6 serving plates.
2. Spoon the dressing over and place a tablespoon of mayonnaise in the center of each salad.

Caribbean Chicken Salad

Ingredients:

- 4 cups chopped green leaf lettuce
- 1 cup chopped red cabbage
- 4 boneless, skinless chicken breast halves
- 1/2 cup teriyaki marinade (store bought)
- 4 cups chopped iceberg lettuce

Pico de gallo:

- 2 tsps. chopped fresh jalapeno pepper, seeded and de?ribbed
- 2 tsps. finely minced fresh cilantro pinch of salt Combine all Ingredients: in a small bowl. Cover and chill.
- 2 medium tomatoes, diced

- 1/2 cup diced spanish onion

Lime dressing:

- 1/4 cup honey
- 11/2 Tbsps. brown sugar twin
- 1 Tbsp. sesame oil
- 1/4 cup Grey Poupon dijon mustard
- 11/2 Tbsp. apple cider vinegar
- 1 1/2 tsps. lime juice

Directions:

1. Blend all the ingredients in a small bowl with an electric mixer, Cover and chill.
2. Marinate the chicken in the teriyaki for at least two hours. Use aresealable plastic bag.
3. Put in fridge. Preheat outdoor or indoor grill. Grill the chicken for 45 mins. per side or until done.

4. Toss the lettuces and cabbage together and divide into 2 large serving size salad bowls.
5. Divide the pico de gallo and pour in equal portions over the two bowls of greens.
6. Slice the grilled chicken into thin strips and divide among bowls. Pour the dressing into two small bowls and serve with the salads.

Balsamic And Bacon Vegetable Medley

Ingredients:

- 3 ounces Brussels sprouts, trimmed and halved
- 3 ounces beets, peeled and chopped
- 3 ounces summer squash or zucchini, chopped
- ¼ cup water
- 1 tablespoon extra-virgin olive oil
- 2 tablespoons balsamic vinegar
- 8 ounces bacon, cooked and crumbled
- 1 small onion, chopped
- 2 bell peppers, seeded and chopped
- 3 ounces carrots, peeled and chopped

- 3 ounces green beans, cut into 1-inch pieces

Directions:

1. Coat a slow cooker generously with cooking spray.
2. Add the bacon, onion, bell peppers, carrots, green beans, Brussels sprouts, beets, and squash to the slow cooker.
3. In a small bowl, mix together the water, olive oil, and vinegar to make a sauce. Pour it over the top of the vegetables.
4. Cook on low for 4 to 6 hours or on high for 2 to 3 hours, or until Brussels sprouts are tender.

Garden Vegetable Soup

Ingredients:

- 4 ounces kale, chopped
- 1 onion, diced
- 1 bell pepper, seeded and diced
- 2 garlic cloves, minced
- 1 tablespoon Italian seasoning
- ½ teaspoon salt
- ¼ teaspoon freshly ground black pepper
- 4 cups Vegetable Broth or store-bought low-sodium vegetable broth
- 1 (15-ounce) can low-sodium or no-salt-added diced tomatoes
- 2 small zucchini, diced

- 2 carrots, peeled and chopped
- 4 ounces green beans, chopped
- 1 bay leaf

Directions:

1. Add the broth, tomatoes, zucchini, carrots, green beans, kale, onion, bell pepper, garlic, Italian seasoning, salt, black pepper, and bay leaf to a slow cooker.
2. Cook on low for 6 to 8 hours or on high for 3 to 4 hours, or until vegetables are soft.
3. Remove the bay leaf prior to serving.

French Onion Soup

Ingredients:

- 2 garlic cloves, minced
- ½ teaspoon salt
- ¼ teaspoon freshly ground black pepper

- 1 bay leaf

- 4 cups low-sodium beef broth

- 4 medium white onions, sliced as thin as possible

- 2 tablespoons unsalted butter

- 4 (1-ounce) slices provolone cheese

Directions:
1. Add the broth, onions, butter, garlic, salt, pepper, and bay leaf to a slow cooker. Stir to mix well.
2. Cook on low for 6 to 8 hours or on high for 3 to 4 hours.
3. Preheat the oven to broil.
4. Ladle the soup into 4 oven-safe soup bowls and place on a baking sheet. Place 1 slice of provolone over the soup in each bowl, and broil for 1 minute, or until the cheese melts.

Raspberry Crumble

Ingredients:

- 1 tablespoon butter
- 1 tablespoon brown sugar
- 1 tablespoon cinnamon
- ¼ tsp cloves
- 2 eggs
- 1 cup raspberries
- 1 cup apple juice
- 1 cup oats

Directions:

1. Preheat oven to 375 F
2. In a bowl combine raspberries, apple slices and apple juice

3. In another bowl combine sugar, spices, oats, butter and mix well
4. Cover apple slices with crumble topping
5. Bake for 45-50 minutes
6. When ready remove and serve

www.ingramcontent.com/pod-product-compliance
Lightning Source LLC
LaVergne TN
LVHW010224070526
838199LV00062B/4719